contents

glamorous wrap

Easy

MATERIALS

Yarn

RED HEART® With Love™ Metallic, 4½oz/127g balls, each approx 200yd/183m (acrylic/metallic) 

- 2 balls in 8410 Charcoal

Crochet Hook

- Size J-10 (6mm) crochet hook, *or size to obtain gauge*

Notions

- Yarn needle

FINISHED MEASUREMENTS

Approx 17"/43cm wide and 72"/183cm long

GAUGE

Gauge is not critical for this project.

WRAP

Ch 66.

Row 1 Tr in 6th ch from hook (beginning ch count as ch-5 space), *ch 3, skip next 4 ch, sc in next ch, ch 3, skip next 4 ch, (tr, ch 5, tr) in next ch; repeat from * across, turn—6 sc and 7 ch-5 spaces.

Row 2 Ch 1, sc in first ch-5 space, *ch 3, (tr, ch 5, tr) in next sc, ch 3, sc in next ch-5 space; repeat from * across, turn—7 sc and 6 ch-5 spaces.

Row 3 Ch 5, tr in first sc, *ch 3, sc in next ch-5 space, ch 3, (tr, ch 5, tr) in next sc; repeat from * across, turn—6 sc and 7 ch-5 spaces.

Repeat Rows 2 and 3 until shawl measures 72"/183cm or desired length. Fasten off.

FINISHING

Weave in ends. •

speckled super scarf

Easy

MATERIALS

Yarn
RED HEART® Super Saver®, 5oz/141g skeins, each approx 236yd/215m (acrylic) (4)
• 3 skeins in 3975 Tourmaline

Crochet Hook
• Size K-10½ (6.5mm) crochet hook, *or size to obtain gauge*

Notions
• Yarn needle

FINISHED MEASUREMENTS
Approx 10.5"/26.5cm wide and 90"/228.5cm long

GAUGE
24 sts (2 ripples) = 7"/18cm; 5 rows = 4"/10cm using size K-10½ (6.5mm) crochet hook.
CHECK YOUR GAUGE.
Use any size hook to obtain gauge.

SPECIAL STITCH
Dc2tog (double crochet 2 together) *Yo, insert hook into next stitch indicated and pull up a loop, yo and draw through 2 loops on hook; repeat from * once more in next stitch indicated, yo and draw through all 3 loops on hook—1 st decrease.

SCARF
Ch 37.
Row 1 (Right Side) Sc in second ch from hook and each across. Turn—36 sc.
Row 2 Ch 1, work in back loops only, sc in each sc across. Turn.
Row 3 Ch 3 (counts as dc throughout), work in back loops only, dc in first st, *dc in next 3 sts [dc2tog in next 2 sts] twice, dc in next 3 sts **, 2 dc in next 2 sts; rep from * across ending at **, 2 dc in last st. Turn—3 ripples made.
Repeat row 3 until piece measures 89"/226cm.
Last 2 rows Ch 1, work in back loops only, sc in each st across. Turn.
Fasten off.

FINISHING
Weave in ends. •

light & lacy shawl

Easy

MATERIALS

Yarn
RED HEART® Fashion Soft™, 5oz/141g balls, each approx 381yd/348m (acrylic) (3)
- 1 ball each in 4650 Artichoke (A), 4604 Navy (B), and 9440 Grey Heather (C)

Crochet Hook
- Size I-9 (5.5mm) crochet hook, *or size to obtain gauge*

Notions
- Yarn needle
- 3 stitch markers

FINISHED MEASUREMENTS
Approx 48"/122cm wide and 24"/61cm tall

GAUGE
14 sts and 6 rows dc = 4"/10cm using size I-9 (5.5mm) crochet hook.
CHECK YOUR GAUGE.
Use any size hook to obtain gauge.

SPECIAL STITCH
Picot Ch 3, slip st in 3rd ch from hook.

SPECIAL TECHNIQUE
Adjustable Ring Wrap yarn into a ring, ensuring that the tail falls behind the working yarn. Grip ring and tail between middle finger and thumb. Insert hook through center of ring, yarn over (with working yarn) and draw up a loop. Work stitches of first round in the ring. After the first round of stitches is worked, pull gently on tail to tighten ring.

NOTE
Use stitch markers to repeat pattern with greater ease: one for first dc of row, one for last dc of row, one for ch 3 space. Move markers as you go.

SHAWL
With A, form an adjustable ring.

Row 1 Ch 3 (counts as dc, here and throughout), (2 dc, ch 3, 3 dc) in ring; turn—6 dc; 1 ch-3 space. Pull tail to close center ring.

Row 2 Ch 3, 2 dc in first st, ch 5, (2 dc, ch 3, 2 dc) in next ch-3 space, ch 5, skip next 2 dc, 3 dc in top of beginning ch-3—10 dc; 1 ch-3 space; 2 ch-5 spaces.

Row 3 Ch 3, 2 dc in first st, ch 5, (sc, ch 5) in each ch-5 space across to next ch-3 space, (2 dc, ch 3, 2 dc) in next ch-3 space, ch 5, (sc, ch 5) in each ch-5 space across to last 3 dc, skip next 2 dc, 3 dc in top of beginning ch-3—10 dc; 1 ch-3 space; 4 ch-5 spaces.

Rows 4–30 Repeat Row 3—10 dc; 1 ch-3 space; 58 ch-5 spaces at end of last row. Fasten off A. Join B.

Rows 31–34 With B, repeat Row 3—10 dc; 1 ch-3 space; 66 ch-5 spaces at end of last row. Fasten off B. Join C.

Row 35 With C, repeat Row 3—10 dc; 1 ch-3 space; 68 ch-5 spaces at end of last row.

Row 36 Ch 3, 2 dc in first st, (sl st, ch 1, 3 sc, ch 1, sl st) in each ch-5 space across to next ch-3 space, (sl st, ch 1, 2 sc, picot, 2 sc, ch 1, sl st) in next ch-3 space, (sl st, ch 1, 3 sc, ch 1, sl st) in each ch-5 space across to last 3 dc, 3 dc in top of beginning ch-3. Fasten off.

FINISHING
Weave in ends. •

snuggle up scarf

Easy

MATERIALS

Yarn
RED HEART® Collage™, 5oz/141g balls, each approx 55yd/50m (acrylic/wool) 
• 5 balls in 9981 Dollhouse

Crochet Hooks
• Size Q (16mm) crochet hook, *or size to obtain gauge*
• Small crochet hook

FINISHED MEASUREMENTS

Approx 8½"/21.5cm wide and 72"/183cm long, excluding fringe

GAUGE

5 dc = 3"/7.5cm; 4 rows = 5"/12.5cm using size Q (16mm) crochet hook.
CHECK YOUR GAUGE.
Use any size hook to obtain gauge.

SPECIAL STITCH

dc5tog [Yarn over, insert hook in next stitch, yarn over and pull up loop, yarn over, draw through 2 loops] 5 times, yarn over, draw through all 6 loops on hook.

SCARF

With larger crochet hook, ch 16.
Row 1 (Right Side) Work 2 dc in 4th ch from hook (beginning ch count as first dc), skip next 2 ch, sc in next ch, skip next 2 ch, 5 dc in next ch, skip next 2 ch, sc in next ch, skip next 2 ch, 3 dc in last ch, turn—11 dc and 2 sc.
Row 2 Ch 1, sc in first dc, ch 2, dc5tog in next 2 dc, sc, and 2 dc, ch 2, sc in next dc, ch 2, dc5tog in next 2 dc, sc, and 2 dc, ch 2, sc in top of beginning ch, turn—2 dc5tog and 3 sc.
Row 3 Ch 3 (counts as first dc here and throughout), 2 dc in first sc, sc in next dc5tog, 5 dc in next sc, sc in next dc5tog, 3 dc in last sc, turn—11 dc and 2 sc.
Row 4 Repeat Row 2.
Repeat Rows 3 and 4 until piece measures 72"/183cm or desired length. Fasten off.

FINISHING

Fringe
Cut 44 strands, each 25"/63.5cm long. Hold 2 strands together and fold in half to form a loop. Working in opposite side of foundation ch, insert large crochet hook from right side through 2nd ch. Place fold on hook and draw fold through, forming a large loop. Thread ends of strands through loop and pull to tighten. Repeat to attach fringe in next 10 ch of Row 1, then repeat to attach 11 fringes centered across sts and ch of last row. Trim ends evenly. With small crochet hook, weave in ends. •

oversized crochet scarf

Easy

MATERIALS

Yarn
RED HEART® Unforgettable®, 3½oz/100g balls, each approx 270yd/247m (acrylic)
• 4 balls in 3962 Sugarcane

Crochet Hook
• Size I-9 (5.5mm) crochet hook, *or size to obtain gauge*

Notions
• Yarn needle

FINISHED MEASUREMENTS
Approx 11"/28cm wide and 92"/234cm long

GAUGE
16 sc = 4"/10cm; 14 rows = 4"/10cm in single crochet using size I-9 (5.5mm) crochet hook.
CHECK YOUR GAUGE.
Use any size hook to obtain gauge.

NOTE
Scarf is worked on the diagonal from one short end to opposite short end, increasing at one side edge and decreasing at opposite side edge every row.

SPECIAL STITCHES
Lch (long chain) Pull up a loop to height of next st.
sc2tog [Draw up a loop in next st] twice, yarn over and draw through all 3 loops on hook.

SCARF
Foundation Row Ch 60, Lch (does not count as a st here and throughout), (dc, sc) in first ch, dc in next ch, *sc in next ch, dc in next ch; repeat from * to last 2 ch, sc2tog in last 2 ch—60 sts.
Row 1 Lch, turn, skip first st, *dc in next dc, sc in next sc; repeat from * to last st, (dc, sc) in last dc.
Row 2 Lch, (dc, sc) in first sc, *dc in next dc, sc in next sc; repeat from * to last 2 sts, sc2tog over last 2 sts.
Repeat Rows 1 and 2 until scarf measures 92"/234cm along one long edge. Fasten off.

FINISHING
Weave in ends. •

genuine pleasure shawl

Easy

MATERIALS

Yarn

RED HEART® Soft®, 4oz/113g balls, each approx 212yd/194m (acrylic) 

- 6 balls in 9440 Light Grey Heather

Crochet Hook

- Size K-10½ (6.5mm) crochet hook, *or size to obtain gauge*

Notions

- Yarn needle

FINISHED MEASUREMENTS

Approx 76½"/194.5cm wide and 37½"/95.5cm long

GAUGE

12 sts = 4"/10cm; 7 rows = 4"/10cm using size K-10½ (6.5mm) crochet hook.
CHECK YOUR GAUGE.
Use any size hook to obtain gauge.

SHAWL

Ch 3; join with slip st in first ch to form a ring

Row 1 (Right Side) Ch 2 (counts as first sc and ch-1 space here and throughout), (sc, ch 1, sc, ch 2, sc, ch 1, 2 sc) in ring, turn—6 sc, 3 ch-1 spaces, and 1 ch-2 space.

Row 2 Ch 2, sc in first sc, ch 1, sc in next ch-1 space, ch 1, (sc, ch 2, sc) in next ch-2 space, ch 1, sc in next ch-1 space, ch 1, sc in last sc, sc in beginning ch-2 space, turn—8 sc, 5 ch-1 spaces, and 1 ch-2 space.

Row 3 Ch 2, sc in first sc, [ch 1, sc in next ch-1 space] 2 times, ch 1, (sc, ch 2, sc) in next ch-2 space, [ch 1, sc in next ch-1 space] 2 times, ch 1, sc in last sc, sc in beginning ch-2 space, turn—10 sc, 7 ch-1 spaces, and 1 ch-2 space.

Row 4 Ch 2, sc in first sc, [ch 1, sc in next ch-1 space] 3 times, ch 1, (sc, ch 2, sc) in next ch-2 space, [ch 1, sc in next ch-1 space] 3 times, ch 1, sc in last sc, sc in beginning ch-2 space, turn—12 sc, 9 ch-1 spaces, and 1 ch-2 space.

Row 5 Ch 3 (counts as first dc and ch-1 space here and throughout), dc in first sc, (ch 1, dc) in each ch-1 space across to next ch-2 space, ch 1, (dc, ch 2, dc) in next ch-2 space, (ch 1, dc) in each ch-1 space across to last sc, ch 1, dc in last sc, dc in beginning ch-2, turn—14 dc, 11 ch-1 spaces, and 1 ch-2 space.

Row 6 Ch 2, sc in first dc, (ch 1, sc) in each ch-1 space across to next ch-2 space, ch 1, (sc, ch 2, sc) in next ch-2 space, (ch 1, sc) in each ch-1 space across to last dc, ch 1, sc in last dc, sc in beginning ch-3 space, turn—16 sc, 13 ch-1 spaces, and 1 ch-2 space.

Row 7 Ch 2, sc in first sc, (ch 1, sc) in each ch-1 space across to next ch-2 space, ch 1, (sc, ch 2, sc) in next ch-2 space, (ch 1, sc) in each ch-1 space across to last sc, ch 1, sc in last sc, sc in beginning ch-2 space, turn—18 sc, 15 ch-1 spaces, and 1 ch-2 space.

Rows 8 and 9 Repeat Rows 5 and 6—22 sc, 19 ch-1 spaces, and 1 ch-2 space.

Rows 10–12 Repeat Row 7—28 sc, 25 ch-1 spaces, and 1 ch-2 space.

Rows 13–18 Repeat Rows 5–7 twice—40 sc, 37 ch-1 spaces, and 1 ch-2 space.

Rows 19–23 Repeat Rows 8–12 once—50 sc, 47 ch-1 spaces, and 1 ch-2 space.

Row 24–78 Repeat Rows 13–23 five times—160 sc, 157 ch-1 spaces, and 1 ch-2 space.

Rows 79–84 Repeat Rows 5–7 twice—172 sc, 169 ch-1 spaces, and 1 ch-2 space.

Row 85 Working in ends of rows, ch 1 (corner made), work 216 sc evenly spaced across top edge to beginning ch-2 space of last row, ch 1 (corner made), slip st in beginning ch-2. Fasten off.

FINISHING

Weave in ends. Block to finished measurements.

Fringe

For each fringe, cut 3 strands, each 10"/25.5cm long. Fold strands in half to form a loop. Insert crochet hook from right side through either corner. Place fold on hook and draw fold through, forming a loop. Thread ends of strands through loop and pull to tighten. Repeat to attach fringe in other corner and in every other ch-1 space across the long side edges of the shawl. Trim ends evenly.

jazzy striping scarf

Easy

MATERIALS

Yarn
RED HEART® Super Saver Stripes™, 5oz/141g skeins, each approx 236yd/215m (acrylic) (5)
- 2 skeins in 4967 Cool Stripe

Crochet Hook
- Size H-8 (5mm) crochet hook, *or size to obtain gauge*

Notions
- Yarn needle

FINISHED MEASUREMENTS
Approx 8½"/22cm wide and 72"/183cm long

GAUGE
13 sts = 4"/10cm; 8 rows = 4"/10cm in pattern using size H-8 (5mm) crochet hook.
CHECK YOUR GAUGE.
Use any size hook to obtain gauge.

SPECIAL STITCHES
V-st (Dc, ch 1, dc) in indicated st or space.

SCARF
Set-up Row Ch 28, V-st in 5th ch from hook, skip 2 ch, 3 dc in next ch, *skip 2 ch, V-st in next ch, skip 2 ch, 3 dc in next ch; rep from * to last 2 ch, skip 1 ch, dc in last ch, turn—4 V-sts, four 3-dc groups, 2 dc.
Pattern Row Ch 3 (counts as 1 dc), *V-st in second dc of first 3-dc group, 3 dc in ch-1 space of next V-st; rep from * to end, dc in top of turning ch, turn.
Repeat pattern row until scarf is 72"/183cm long. Fasten off.

FINISHING
Weave in ends. •

summer of love shawl

Intermediate

MATERIALS

Yarn
RED HEART® Boutique Unforgettable™, 3½oz/100g balls, each approx 270yd/247m (acrylic)
• 3 balls in 3977 Sunrise

Crochet Hook
• Size J-10 (6mm) crochet hook, *or size to obtain gauge*

Notions
• Yarn needle

FINISHED MEASUREMENTS

Approx 64"/162.5cm across top edge and 38"/96.5cm long, excluding edging

GAUGE

3 pattern repeats and 1 sc = 4"/10cm (one pattern repeat consists of one double Love knot and one single crochet); 5 rows = 4" (10 cm) using size J-10 (6mm) crochet hook.
CHECK YOUR GAUGE.
Use any size hook to obtain gauge.

SPECIAL STITCHES

dLk (double Love knot) [Pull loop up ¾"/2cm, yo and draw through loop, insert hook under back strand of loop, yo and pull up a loop, yo and draw through 2 loops] twice.
fan 8 tr in end of indicated row.
Lk (Love knot) = Pull loop up ¾"/2cm, yo and draw through loop (long chain), insert hook under back strand of loop, yo and pull up a loop, yo and draw through 2 loops (sc made in back of long ch).

SPECIAL TECHNIQUE

Fsc (Foundation single crochet) This technique creates a foundation chain and a row of single crochet stitches in one.

Step 1 Place a slipknot on hook, ch 2, insert hook in 2nd ch from hook and draw up a loop; yarn over and draw through one loop on hook (the "chain"); yarn over and draw through 2 loops on hook (the "single crochet").

Step 2 Insert hook into the "chain" of the previous stitch and draw up a loop, yarn over and draw through one loop on hook (the "chain"), yarn over and draw through 2 loops on hook (the "single crochet"). Repeat for the length of foundation row.

NOTES

1) Shawl is worked from neck edge down, decreasing one double Love knot in each row.
2) A Love knot is made from two stitches: a long chain and a single crochet worked into the back bar of the chain.
3) When instructed to work into the second single crochet of a double Love knot, work into the single crochet centered between the two knots.
4) Edging is worked in rounds with right side facing.

SHAWL

Foundation Row Work 200 Fsc, do not turn—200 Fsc.
Row 1 (Wrong Side) DLk, working in opposite side of Foundation Row, skip first 3 sts, sc in next st, *dLk, skip next 3 sts, sc in next st; repeat from * across, turn—50 dLks.
Row 2 (Right Side) Lk, sc in 2nd sc of first dLk, *dLk, sc in 2nd sc of next dLk; repeat from * to last dLk; leave last dLk unworked, turn—49 dLks.
Row 3 Lk, sc in 2nd sc of first dLk, *dLk, sc in 2nd sc of next dLk; repeat from * to last dLk; leave last Lk unworked, turn—48 dLks.
Rows 4–48 Repeat Row 3—3 dLks.
Row 49 Lk, sc in 2nd sc of first dLk, dLk, sc in 2nd sc of next dLk; leave last Lk unworked, turn—2 dLks.
Row 50 Lk, sc in 2nd sc of first dLk, dLk, sc in 2nd sc of next dLk, do not turn—1 dLk.

Edging

Round 1 (Right Side) Ch 1, working in ends of rows across first side, fan in Row 49, sc in next row, *fan in next row, sc in next row *; repeat from * to * to Row 1, fan in Row 1, skip Foundation Row; working in Foundation Row, sc in each st across; working in ends of rows across other side, skip Foundation Row, repeat from * to * across to Row 49, fan in Row 49; working in Row 50, sc in first sc, fan in 2nd sc of dLk, slip st in last sc, do not join or turn—51 fans and 250 sc.
Round 2 Ch 1, (sc in first tr, dc in next tr, [ch 1, dc in next tr] 6 times) of first fan, sc in next sc, *(sc in first tr, dc in next tr, [ch

1, dc in next tr] 6 times) of next fan, sc in next sc *; repeat from * to * to top edge; working across top edge, **ch 1, skip next sc, hdc in next sc, repeat from ** across to last sc, skip last sc, (dc in next tr, [ch 1, dc in next tr] 7 times) of next fan, sc in next sc; repeat from * to * to last fan, (sc in first tr, dc in next tr, [ch 1, dc in next tr] 6 times) of last fan, sc in last sc; join with slip st in first sc—357 dc, 99 hdc, 102 sc, and 407 ch-1 spaces.

Round 3 Ch 1, sc in first dc, [2 sc in next ch-1 space] 6 times, *skip next dc, sc in next sc, slip st in next sc, sc in next dc, [2 sc in next ch-1 space] 6 times *; repeat from * to * 23 times, [2 sc in next ch-1 space] 108 times; repeat from * to * around to last dc, skip last dc, sc in last sc; join with slip st in last slip st of Round 2. Fasten off.

FINISHING

Weave in ends. •

daydream scarf

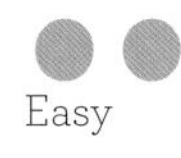
Easy

MATERIALS

Yarn
RED HEART® Dreamy™, 8⅘oz/250g balls, each approx 466yd/426m (acrylic)
• 2 balls in 8341 Grey

Crochet Hook
• Size J-10 (6mm) crochet hook, *or size to obtain gauge*

Notions
• Yarn needle
• 8"/20cm x 3"/7.5cm piece of heavy cardboard

FINISHED MEASUREMENTS

Approx 12"/30cm wide and 85"/216cm long

GAUGE

2 repeats = 4"/10cm; 6 rows = 4"/10cm using size J-10 (6mm) crochet hook.
CHECK YOUR GAUGE.
Use any size hook to obtain gauge.

SCARF

Ch 38.

Row 1 Sc in 2nd ch from hook, *skip 2 ch, 5 dc in next ch (scallop made), skip 2 ch, sc in next ch; repeat from * 5 times; turn—7 sc, six 5-dc scallops.

Row 2 Ch 5 (counts as first dc, ch 2), *skip 2 dc, sc in 3rd dc, ch 2, skip 2 dc, dc in sc, ch 2; repeat from * across, ending dc in last sc; turn—7 dc, 6 sc, 12 ch-2 loops.

Row 3 Ch 1, sc in dc, *skip 2 ch, 5 dc in sc, skip 2 ch, sc in dc; repeat from * across, ending sc in 3rd ch of last ch-5; turn—7 sc, six 5-dc scallops.

Repeat Rows 2 and 3 until Scarf measures 85"/216cm. Fasten off.

FINISHING

Tassels (Make 4)

Cut two 10"/25.5cm strands, set aside. Wrap yarn around cardboard 35 times. Thread 10"/25.5cm strand under top edge and tie top end of wrapped yarn tightly. Do not cut tails. Cut across bottom ends of yarn. Wrap remaining 10"/25.5cm strand around top of tassel, 1"/2.5cm from top knot, and tie tightly. Thread ends of this tie into center of tassel. Trim ends of tassel evenly to desired length. Tie tassel to each corner of scarf with top tails.

Weave in ends. •

skinny scarf

Beginner

MATERIALS

Yarn
RED HEART® Hopscotch™, 4oz/113g balls, each approx 210yd/193m (acrylic) (4)
• 1 ball in 7959 Bicycle

Crochet Hook
• Size K-10½ (6.5mm) crochet hook, *or size to obtain gauge*

Notions
• Yarn needle

FINISHED MEASUREMENTS

Approx 4"/10cm wide and 84"/213cm long

GAUGE

4 sts = 4"/10cm; 7 rows = 4"/10cm in pattern using size K-10 1/2 (6.5mm) crochet hook.
CHECK YOUR GAUGE.
Use any size hook to obtain gauge.

SPECIAL STITCH

GS (granny stitch) Work 3 dc into same st.

SCARF

Ch 10.
Row 1 Skip 3 ch, GS into next ch, *skip 2 ch, GS into next ch; repeat from * once more, ch 2, turn.
Row 2 *GS in space between the next 2 GS of previous row; repeat from * once more, GS in space between the last GS of previous row and turning ch; ch 2, turn.
Repeat Row 2 until scarf measures 84"/213cm long.
Fasten off.

FINISHING

Weave in ends. •

lacy pineapple shawl

Intermediate

MATERIALS

Yarn

RED HEART® Heart & Sole®, 1¾oz/50g balls, each approx 187yd/171m (wool/nylon)

- 4 balls in 3540 Purple

Crochet Hook

- Size F-5 (3.75mm) crochet hook, *or size to obtain gauge*

Notions

- Removable stitch markers
- Yarn needle

FINISHED MEASUREMENTS

Approx 68"/173cm across and 34"/86cm in length at center

GAUGE

Rows 1–10 = 13"/33cm x 8½"/21.5cm using size F-5 (3.75mm) crochet hook.
CHECK YOUR GAUGE.
Use any size hook to obtain gauge.

SPECIAL STITCHES

beg shell Ch 3 (counts as 1 dc), (dc, ch 2, 2 dc) in same space as last slip st.

shell (2 dc, ch 2, 2 dc) in indicated st or space.

SHAWL

Ch 4, and slip st in first ch to form a ring.

Row 1 (Right Side) Ch 1, 5 sc in ring, turn.

Row 2 Ch 6 (counts as 1 dc and 3 ch), dc in first sc, *ch 3, skip next sc, (dc, ch 3, dc) in next dc; repeat from * once more, turn.

Row 3 Slip st in first dc and in first ch-3 space, beg shell, *ch 3, (dc, ch 3, dc) in next ch-3 space, ch 3, shell in next ch-3 space; repeat from * once more, turn.

Row 4 Slip st in each of first 2 dc and in first ch-2 space, beg shell, *ch 3, skip next ch-3 space, (dc, ch 3) 5 times in next ch-3 space, skip next ch-3 space, shell in next ch-2 space; repeat from * once more, turn.

Row 5 Slip st in each of first 2 dc and in first ch-2 space, ch 6 (counts as 1 dc and 3 ch), shell in first ch-2 space, *ch 3, skip next ch-3 space, (sc, ch 5) in each of next 3 ch-3 spaces, sc in next ch-3 space, ch 3, skip next ch-3 space *, (shell, ch 3, shell) in next ch-2 space, repeat from * to * once more, (shell, ch 3, dc) in last ch-2 space, turn.

Row 6 Slip st in first dc and in first ch-3 space, beg shell, ch 2, shell in next ch-2 space, *ch 3, skip next ch-3 space, (sc, ch 5) in each of next 2 ch-5 spaces, sc in next ch-5 space, ch 3, skip next ch-3 space *, (shell, ch 2) in each of next 2 spaces, shell in next ch-2 space, repeat from * to * once more, shell in next ch-2 space, ch 2, shell in last space, turn.

Mark first, last, and center spaces. Move markers up to corresponding spaces after each row.

Row 7 Slip st to first space, beg shell, *ch 3, skip next space, (dc, ch 3) 5 times in next ch-2 space, [skip next ch-3 space, sc in next ch-5 space, ch 5, sc in next ch-5 space, ch 3, (dc, ch 3) 5 times in next ch-2 space, ch 3] to last space before marked space *, skip next space, shell in center space, repeat from * to * once more, skip next space, shell in last space, turn.

Row 8 Slip St in each of first 2 dc and in first ch-2 space, ch 6 (counts as 1 dc and 3 ch), shell in first ch-2 space, *ch 3, skip next ch-3 space, (sc, ch 5) in each of next 3 ch-3 spaces, sc in next ch-3 space, ch 3, skip next ch-3 space, [shell in next ch-5 space, ch 3, skip next ch-3 space, (sc, ch 5) in each of next 3 ch-3 spaces, sc in next ch-3 space, ch 3] to marked space *, (shell, ch 3, shell) in center space, repeat from * to * once more, (shell, ch 3, dc) in last ch-2 space, turn.

Row 9 Slip st in first dc and in first space, ch 6 (counts as 1 dc and 3 ch), dc in first space, *ch 3, shell in next ch-2 space, ch 3, [skip next ch-3 space, (sc, ch 5) in each of next 2 ch-5 spaces, sc in next ch-5 space, ch 3, skip next ch- 3 space, shell in next ch-2 space, ch 3] to marked space *, (dc, ch 3, dc) in center space, repeat from * to * once more, (dc, ch 3, dc) in last space, turn.

Repeat Rows 7–9 twelve more times.

lacy pineapple shawl

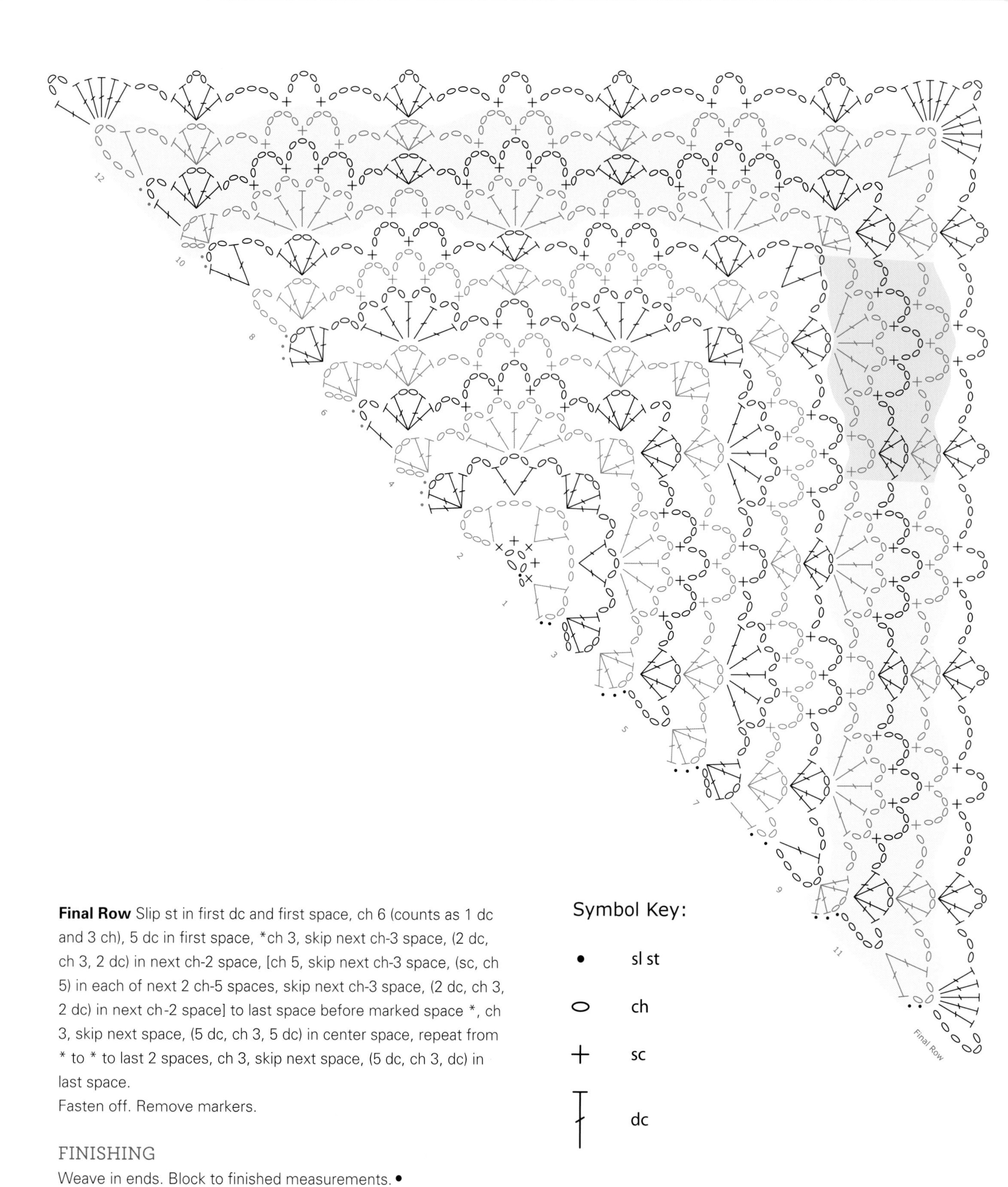

Final Row Slip st in first dc and first space, ch 6 (counts as 1 dc and 3 ch), 5 dc in first space, *ch 3, skip next ch-3 space, (2 dc, ch 3, 2 dc) in next ch-2 space, [ch 5, skip next ch-3 space, (sc, ch 5) in each of next 2 ch-5 spaces, skip next ch-3 space, (2 dc, ch 3, 2 dc) in next ch-2 space] to last space before marked space *, ch 3, skip next space, (5 dc, ch 3, 5 dc) in center space, repeat from * to * to last 2 spaces, ch 3, skip next space, (5 dc, ch 3, dc) in last space.

Fasten off. Remove markers.

Symbol Key:

- • sl st
- 0 ch
- + sc
- dc

FINISHING

Weave in ends. Block to finished measurements. •

wrapped in elegance

Intermediate

MATERIALS

Yarn
Red Heart® Boutique Unforgettable®, 3½oz/100g balls, each approx 270yd/247m (acrylic) (4)
• 3 balls in 3952 Tealberry

Crochet Hooks
• One each size F-5 (3.75mm) and J-10 (6.0mm) crochet hook, *or sizes to obtain gauge*

Notions
• Yarn needle

FINISHED MEASUREMENTS

Approx 17"/43cm wide and 60"/152.5cm long

GAUGE

2 pattern repeats = 4"/10cm (one pattern repeat consists of one herringbone half double crochet and one chain); 14 rows = 4"/10cm using larger crochet hook.
CHECK YOUR GAUGE.
Use any size hook to obtain gauge.

SPECIAL STITCHES

beg 3-tr Cl (beginning 3 treble crochet cluster) Ch 3, [yarn over] twice, insert hook in indicated space, yarn over and pull up a loop, [yarn over and draw through 2 loops on hook] twice; *[yarn over] twice, insert hook in same space, yarn over and pull up a loop, [yarn over and draw through 2 loops on hook] twice, yarn over and draw through all 4 loops on hook.
fan [ch 3, 3-tr Cl] 3 times in indicated space.
hhdc (herringbone half double crochet) Yarn over, insert hook in indicated stitch, yarn over, draw through stitch and first loop on hook (2 loops on hook), yarn over, draw through both loops on hook.
reverse sc (reverse single crochet) Work single crochet in opposite direction from which you would usually work (left to right if you are right-handed and right to left if you are left-handed). This stitch is also known as crab stitch. It creates a rope-like twisted single crochet edging.

3-tr Cl (3 treble crochet cluster) [Yarn over] twice, insert hook in indicated stitch, yarn over and pull up a loop, [yarn over and draw through 2 loops on hook] twice; *[yarn over] twice, insert hook in same stitch, yarn over and pull up a loop, [yarn over and draw through 2 loops on hook] twice; repeat from * once, yarn over and draw through all 4 loops on hook.

NOTES

1) Center panel of wrap is worked in turned rows. Side panels are worked across each end of center panel.
2) Four rows of edging are worked across side and bottom edges of each side panel and across bottom of center panel. Edging finishes in a round around entire piece and with a row of reverse single crochet across the top edge.

SHAWL

Center Panel

With larger hook, ch 164.
Row 1 (Right Side) Hhdc in 3rd ch from hook (beginning ch count as first hhdc), *ch 1, skip next ch, hhdc in next ch; repeat from * across to last ch, hhdc in last ch, turn—83 hhdc and 80 ch-1 spaces.
Rows 2–40 Ch 2 (counts as first hhdc here and throughout), hhdc in next st, *ch 1, skip next hhdc, hhdc in next ch-1 space; repeat from * across to beginning ch, hhdc in top of beginning ch, turn. Do not fasten off or turn at end of last row.

First Side Panel

Row 1 Ch 3 (counts as hhdc, ch 1 here and throughout), working across ends of rows, hhdc in next row, [ch 1, hhdc in next row] 3 times, *skip next row, [ch 1, hhdc in next row] 4 times; repeat from * across, turn—33 hhdc and 32 ch-1 spaces.
Rows 2–20 Ch 2, hhdc in first ch-1 space, (ch 1, hhdc) in each ch-1 space across, turn.
Fasten off.

2nd Side Panel

Row 1 Hold center panel with wrong side facing, join yarn with slip st in unworked end of first row, ch 3, working across ends of rows, hhdc in next row, [ch 1, hhdc in next row] 3 times, *skip next row, [ch 1, hhdc in next row] 4 times; repeat from * across, turn—33 hhdc and 32 ch-1 spaces.
Rows 2–20 Repeat Rows 2–20 of first side panel. Do not fasten off. Change to smaller hook.

Edging

Row 1 (Right Side) Ch 5 (counts as sc, ch 4 here and throughout), sc in first st, *ch 6, skip next 3 ch-1 spaces, (sc, ch 4, sc) in next ch-1 space *; repeat from * to * 7 times; working in ends of rows across bottom edge of 2nd side panel, [ch 10, skip next 5 rows, (sc, ch 4, sc) in next row] 3 times; working across center panel, ch 10, skip next 4 ch-1 spaces, (sc, ch 4, sc) in next ch-1 space, [ch 10, skip next 5 ch-1 spaces, (sc, ch 4, sc) in next ch-1 space] 13 times; working in ends of rows across first side panel, [ch 10, skip next 5 rows, (sc, ch 4, sc) in next row] 3 times; working across short edge of first side panel; repeat from * to * 8 times, turn—37 ch-4 spaces.
Rows 2 and 3 Ch 1, slip st in first ch-4 space, (ch 5, sc) in same space, [ch 6, (sc, ch 4, sc) in next ch-4 space] 8 times, [ch 10, (sc, ch 4, sc) in next ch-4 space] 20 times, [ch 6, (sc, ch 4, sc) in next ch-4 space] 8 times, turn.
Row 4 Ch 1, slip st in first ch-4 space, (ch 5, sc) in same space, [ch 6, (sc, ch 4, sc) in next ch-4 space] 7 times, [(sc, ch 4, sc)] 3 times in next ch-4 space, [ch 10, (sc, ch 4, sc) in next ch-4 space] 19 times, [(sc, ch 4, sc)] 3 times in next ch-4 space, [ch 6, (sc, ch 4, sc) in next ch-4 space] 8 times, turn—41 ch-4 spaces.
Round 5 Sl st in first ch-4 space, (beg 3-tr Cl, [ch 3, 3-tr Cl] twice) in same space (counts as first fan), fan in next 7 ch-4 spaces, *ch 3, 3-tr Cl in next ch-4 space, fan in next ch-4 space, ch 3, 3-tr Cl in next ch-4 space *, fan in next 19 ch-4 spaces; repeat from * to * once, fan in last 7 ch-4 spaces, [slip st in vertical bar of last tr made] twice; working in ends of rows across first side panel, 2 sc in next 4 ch-4 spaces, 2 sc in next row, [skip next row, 2 sc in next row] 9 times; working in center panel, 2 sc in each ch-1 space across; working in ends of rows across 2nd side panel, 2 sc in first 2 rows, [skip next row, 2 sc in next row] 8 times, skip next row, 2 sc in last 4 ch-4 spaces, do not join or turn—37 fans, four 3-tr Cls, and 222 sc.
Last Row Ch 1, reverse sc in first sc, *skip next sc, reverse sc in next sc; repeat from * across—111 sc. Fasten off.

FINISHING

Weave in ends.●

cici's ombre super scarf

Easy

MATERIALS

Yarn
RED HEART® Super Saver Ombre™, 10oz/283g skeins, each approx 482yd/440m (acrylic)
• 2 skeins in 3985 Deep Teal

Crochet Hook
• Size I-9 (5.5mm) crochet hook, *or size to obtain gauge*

Notions
• Yarn needle

SIZES
Small/Medium (Large/Extra Large, 2X/3X).

FINISHED MEASUREMENTS
Approx 10"/25.5cm wide and 90"/229cm long

GAUGE
5 stitch repeats = 4"/10cm; 10 rows = 4"/10cm in pattern stitch using size I-9 (5.5mm) crochet hook.
CHECK YOUR GAUGE.
Use any size hook to obtain gauge.

NOTE
When joining new skein, pick up new skein within same color section as old skein.

PATTERN STITCH
(multiple of 3 ch + 2)
Foundation Row Work (sc, ch 2, sc) in 3rd ch from hook, *skip next 2 ch, (sc, ch 2, sc) in next ch; repeat from * across to last ch, hdc in last ch.
Row 1 Ch 3 (counts as dc here and throughout), turn, *3 dc in next ch-2 space (shell made); repeat from * across, dc in top of turning ch.
Row 2 Ch 2 (counts as hdc here and throughout), turn, *(sc, ch 2, sc) in 2nd dc of next shell; repeat from * across, hdc in top of turning ch.
Repeat Rows 1–2 for pattern st.

SCARF
Ch 41.
Beginning with Foundation Row, work in pattern st until piece measures 90"/229cm from beginning. Fasten off.

FINISHING
Weave in ends. •

wrap-ture shawl

Easy

MATERIALS

Yarn

RED HEART® Evermore™, 3½oz/100g balls, each approx 89yd/81m (acrylic/wool) 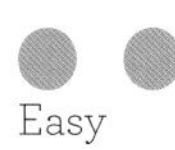

- 7 balls in 9935 Mulberry

Crochet Hook

- Size M-13 (9mm) crochet hook, *or size to obtain gauge*

Notions

- Stitch marker

FINISHED MEASUREMENTS

Approx 63"/160cm at widest point and 37"/94cm at longest point

GAUGE

11 dc = 6"/15cm; 7 rows = 6"/15cm in double crochet using size M-13 (9mm) crochet hook.

CHECK YOUR GAUGE.

Use any size hook to obtain gauge.

NOTE

Shawl is worked from center of longest edge, increasing sts in center space, to end with sts worked along two side edges. An edging is worked around entire finished piece.

SHAWL

Ch 5.

Row 1 (Wrong Side) (Dc, ch 1) 4 times in 5th ch from hook (skipped 4 ch count as first dc and ch-1 space), dc in same ch—6 dc and 5 ch-1 spaces. Place marker in center ch-1 space and move it up to next center space as you work each row.

Row 2 Ch 4 (counts as dc, ch 1 here and throughout), turn, [dc in next ch-1 space, ch 1] to marked center space, (dc, ch 2, dc) in center space, ch 1, [dc in next space, ch 1] to last st, dc in 3rd ch of beginning ch-4—6 ch-1 spaces and 1 ch-2 corner space.

Row 3 Ch 4, turn, [dc in next space, ch 1] to center space, ([dc, ch 1] 3 times, dc) in center space, ch 1, [dc in next space, ch 1] to last st, dc in 3rd ch of beginning ch-4.

Row 4 Ch 4, turn, [dc in next ch-1 space, ch 1] to center space, (dc, ch 2, dc) in center space, ch 1, [dc in next space, ch 1] to last st, dc in 3rd ch of beginning ch-4.

Row 5 Repeat Row 3.

Row 6 Ch 3 (counts as dc here and throughout), turn, 2 dc in each ch-1 space to center space, (2 dc, ch 1, 2 dc) in center space, 2 dc in each ch-1 space to last st, dc in 3rd ch of beginning ch-4

Rows 7–10 Ch 3, turn, dc in same st, dc in each dc to center space, (2 dc, ch 1, 2 dc) in center space, dc in each st to last st, 2 dc in top of beginning ch-3—62 dc and 1 center ch-1 space at end of Row 10.

Row 11 Ch 4, turn, dc in same st, ch 1, [dc in next dc, ch 1, skip next dc] to center space, (dc, ch 2, dc) in center space, [ch 1, skip next dc, dc in next dc] to last st, ch 1, (dc, ch 1, dc) in top of beginning ch-3.

Rows 12–20 Repeat Rows 2–10.

Row 21 Repeat Row 11.

Rows 22–28 Repeat Rows 2–8.

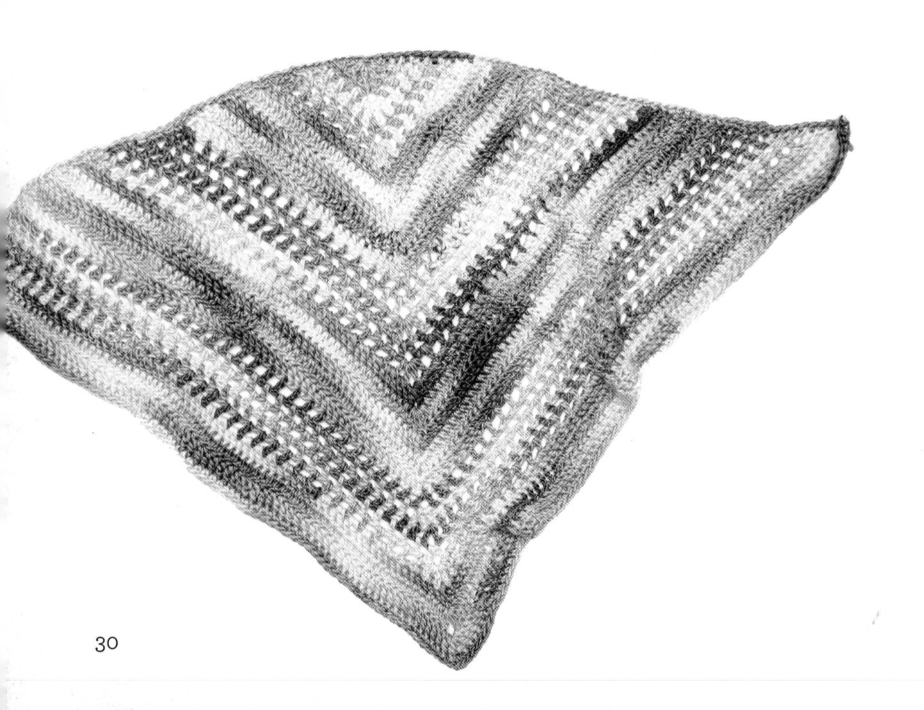

Edging

With right side facing, ch 1, do not turn, 2 sc in same st, working long edge, sc evenly spaced along long edge to opposite corner, 2 sc in corner st, turn to work along side edge, sc evenly to center ch-space, 3 sc in center space, working along opposite side edge, sc evenly to first st, slip st in first st to join. Fasten off.

FINISHING

Weave in ends. •

let's party poncho

Intermediate

MATERIALS

Yarn
RED HEART® With Love™ Metallic, 4½oz/127g balls, each approx 204yd/186m (acrylic/metallic) (4)
- 6 (7, 8) balls in 8524 Teal

Crochet Hook
- Size I-9 (5.5mm) crochet hook, *or size to obtain gauge*

Notions
- Removable stitch markers
- Yarn needle

SIZES

Small/Medium (Large/1X, 2X/3X).

FINISHED MEASUREMENTS

To fit bust 32–38 (40–46, 48–54)"/81.5–86.5 (101.5–117, 122–137)cm
Length (shoulder to lower edge) 30 (31, 31)"/76 (78.5, 78.5)cm
Side length 20"/51cm
Body width 29 (34, 39)"/73.5 (86.5, 99) cm
Width (lower edge) 27 (31½, 36)"/68.5 (80, 91.5)cm

GAUGE

1 pattern repeat = 2½"/6.5cm; 8 rows = 4"/10cm in Lace Pattern using size I-9 (5.5mm) crochet hook.
CHECK YOUR GAUGE.
Use any size hook to obtain gauge.

SPECIAL STITCHES

2-dc Cl (2-double crochet cluster) Yarn over, insert hook in indicated stitch, yarn over and pull up loop, yarn over, draw through 2 loops on hook (2 loops remain on hook); yarn over, insert hook in same stitch, yarn over and pull up loop, yarn over, draw through 2 loops, yarn over, draw through all 3 loops on hook.
dc2tog [Yarn over, insert hook in next stitch, yarn over and pull up loop, yarn over, draw through 2 loops] 2 times, yarn over, draw through all 3 loops on hook.
edging shell (Sc, ch 1, 3 dc, ch 1, sc) in indicated stitch or space.
shell 5 dc in indicated stitch or space.

LACE PATTERN

Row 1 (Right Side) Ch 3 (counts as first dc here and throughout), dc in next dc, ch 2, working in first shell, dc in next dc, [2 dc in next dc, dc in next dc] twice, *ch 3, sc in next sc, ch 3, working in next shell, dc in first dc, [2 dc in next dc, dc in next dc] twice; repeat from * across to last 2 sts, ch 2, dc in last dc, dc in top of beginning ch, turn.
Row 2 Ch 3, dc in next dc, 2-dc Cl in next dc, [ch 3, skip next dc, 2-dc Cl in next dc] 3 times, *ch 2, 2-dc Cl in next dc, [ch 3, skip next dc, 2-dc Cl in next dc] 3 times; repeat from * across to last 2 sts, dc in last dc, dc in top of beginning ch, turn.
Row 3 Ch 3, dc in next dc, ch 2, [sc in next ch-3 space, ch 2, (sc, ch 3, sc) in next ch-3 space, ch 2, sc in next ch-3 space *, ch 3] across to last 2 sts, ending last repeat at *, ch 2, dc in last dc, dc in top of beginning ch, turn.
Row 4 Ch 3, dc in next dc, *ch 3, shell in next ch-3 space, ch 3, sc in next ch-3 space; repeat from * across to last last 2 sts, ch 3, dc in last dc, dc in top of beginning ch, turn.
Repeat Rows 1–4 for Lace Pattern.

NOTE

Poncho is made from 2 panels sewn together at neck and shoulder lines. Sleeves hang open and are not sewn closed across bottom or side seams.

PONCHO

Front/Back Panel (Make 2)

Ch 105 (125, 145).
Foundation Row (Wrong Side) Dc in 4th ch from hook (beginning ch count as first dc), ch 3, skip next 4 ch, shell in next ch, [ch 3, skip next 4 ch, sc in next ch, ch 3, skip next 4 ch, shell in next ch] across to last 6 ch, ch 3, skip next 4 ch, dc in last 2 ch, turn—2 dc at each end, 10 (12, 14) shells, 9 (11, 13) sc, 20 (24, 28) ch-3 spaces.
Rows 1–28 Work Lace Pattern Rows 1–4 seven times.
Rows 29–31 Repeat Rows 1–3—2 dc at each end, 22 (26, 30) ch-2 spaces, 19 (23, 27) ch-3 spaces at end of Row 31.

Shape Sleeves

Row 1 (Wrong Side) Ch 3, skip next dc, 2 dc in next ch-2 space, shell in

next ch-3 space, [ch 3, sc in next ch-3 space, ch 3, shell in next ch-3 space] 9 (11, 13) times, 2 dc in last ch-2 space, skip next dc, dc in top of beginning ch, turn—3 dc at each end, 10 (12, 14) dc, 9 (11, 13) sc. Place marker at each end of row for seam.

Row 2 (Right Side) Ch 3, dc2tog, working in next shell, dc2tog, dc in next dc, 2 dc in next dc, dc in next dc, *ch 3, sc in next sc, ch 3, working in next shell, dc in first dc, [2 dc in next dc, dc in next dc] twice; repeat from * 7 (9, 11) times, ch 3, sc in next sc, ch 3, dc in next dc, 2 dc in next dc, dc in next dc, [dc2tog] twice; leave beginning ch unworked, turn—69 (83, 97) dc and 9 (11, 13) sc.

Row 3 Ch 1, skip first dc, sc in next dc, [ch 3, skip next dc, 2 dc-cl in next dc] twice, *ch 2, 2-dc Cl in next dc, [ch 3, skip next dc, 2 dc cl in next dc] 3 times; repeat from * 7 (9, 11) times, ch 2, [2-dc Cl in next dc, ch 3, skip next dc] twice, sc in next dc; leave last dc unworked, turn—28 (34, 40) ch-3 spaces.

Row 4 Ch 3, dc in first ch-3 space, ch 2, sc in next ch-3 space, [ch 3, sc in next ch-3 space, ch 2, (sc, ch 3, sc) in next ch-3 space, ch 2, sc in next ch-3 space] across to last 2 ch-3 spaces, ch 3, sc in next ch-3 space, ch 2, dc in last ch-3 space, turn—18 (22, 26) ch-3 spaces.

Row 5 Ch 3, sc in first ch-3 space, [ch 3, shell in next ch-3 space, ch 3, sc in next ch-3 space] across, turn—8 (10, 12) shells and 9 (11, 13) sc.

Row 6 Ch 3, 2-dc Cl in first ch-3 space, working in first shell, dc2tog, dc in next dc, 2 dc in next dc, dc in last dc, ch 3, sc in next sc, *ch 3, working in next shell, dc in first dc, [2 dc in next dc, dc in next dc] twice, ch 3, sc in next sc; repeat from * across to last shell, ch 3, working in last shell, dc in first dc, 2 dc in next dc, dc in next dc, dc2tog, 2-dc Cl in next ch-3 space; leave last ch-3 space unworked, turn—54 (68, 82) dc.

Row 7 Ch 1, skip first dc, sc in next dc, [ch 3, skip next dc, 2 dc-cl in next dc] twice, *ch 2, 2-dc Cl in next dc, [ch 3, skip next dc, 2 dc cl in next dc] 3 times; repeat from * 5 (7, 9) times, ch 2, [2-dc Cl in next dc, ch 3, skip next dc] twice, sc in next dc; leave remaining dc unworked, turn—22 (28, 34) ch-3 spaces.

Rows 8–10 Repeat Rows 4–6—40 (54, 68) dc at end of Row 10.

Row 11 Ch 1, skip first dc, sc in next dc, [ch 3, skip next dc, 2 dc-cl in next dc] twice, *ch 2, 2-dc Cl in next dc, [ch 3, skip next dc, 2-dc Cl in next dc] 3 times; repeat from * 3 (5, 7) times, ch 2, [2-dc Cl in next dc, ch 3, skip next dc] twice, sc in next dc, turn—5 (7, 9) ch-2 spaces and 16 (22, 28) ch-3 spaces.

NECKLINE

Size Small/Medium Only

Left Neck Shaping

Row 1 (Right Side) Ch 3, dc in first ch-3 space, 3 dc in next ch-3 space, 2 dc in next ch-2 space, 3 dc in next ch-3 space, dc in next ch-3 space; leave remaining ch spaces unworked, turn—11 dc. Place marker on 12th ch space from last ch-3 space worked.

Rows 2–5 Ch 3, dc2tog, dc in each remaining dc; leave beginning ch unworked, turn—3 dc.

Fasten off.

Right Neck Shaping

Row 1 (Right Side) With right side facing, join with slip st in marked ch-3 space, ch 3, 3 dc in next ch-3 space, 2 dc in next ch-2 space, 3 dc in next ch-3 space, dc in next ch-3 space, turn—11 dc.

Rows 2–5 Repeat Rows 2–5 of left neck shaping. Fasten off.

Size Large/1X Only

Left Neck Shaping

Row 1 (Right Side) Ch 3, dc in first ch-3 space, 3 dc in next ch-3 space, 2 dc in next ch-2 space, 3 dc in next 2 ch-3 spaces, 2-dc Cl in next 2 ch spaces, dc in next ch-3 space; leave remaining ch spaces unworked, turn—16 dc. Place marker on 10th ch space from last ch-3 space worked.

Row 2 Ch 3, dc2tog, dc in each remaining st; leave beginning ch unworked, turn—14 dc.

Rows 3–5 Ch 3, dc2tog, dc in each dc across to last 2 dc, dc2tog; leave beginning ch unworked, turn—5 dc.

Row 6 Ch 3, dc in next st, dc2tog over next 2 sts; leave beginning ch unworked—3 dc. Fasten off.

Right Neck Shaping

Row 1 (Right Side) With right side facing, join with slip st in marked ch-3 space, ch 3, 2-dc Cl in next 2 ch spaces, 3 dc in next 2 ch-3 spaces, 2 dc in next ch-2 space, 3 dc in next ch-3 space, 2 dc in last ch-3 space, turn—16 dc.

Row 2 Ch 3, dc2tog, dc in next 10 dc, dc2tog, turn—13 dc.

Rows 3–5 Repeat Rows 3–5 of left neck shaping—4 dc.
Row 6 Ch 3, dc in next 2 sts; leave beginning ch unworked—3 dc. Fasten off.

Size 2X/3X Only

Left Neck Shaping

Row 1 (Right Side) Ch 3, dc in first ch-3 space, 3 dc in next ch-3 space, 2 dc in next ch-2 space, 3 dc in next 3 ch-3 spaces, 2-dc Cl in next 3 ch spaces, dc in next ch-3 space; leave remaining ch spaces unworked, turn—20 dc. Place marker on 18th ch space from last ch-3 space worked.
Rows 2 and 3 Ch 3, dc2tog, dc in each dc across to last 2 dc, dc2tog; leave beginning ch unworked, turn—14 dc.
Row 4 Ch 3, [dc2tog, dc in next 3 dc] twice, dc2tog; leave beginning ch unworked, turn—10 dc.
Row 5 Ch 3, dc2tog, dc in next 4 dc, dc2tog; leave beginning ch unworked, turn—7 dc.
Row 6 Ch 3, dc2tog, dc in next dc, dc2tog; leave beginning ch unworked—4 dc. Fasten off.

Right Neck Shaping

Row 1 (Right Side) With right side facing, join with slip st in marked ch-3 space, ch 3, 2-dc Cl in next 2 ch-3 spaces, 2-dc Cl in next ch-2 space, 3 dc in next 3 ch-3 spaces, 2 dc in next ch-2 space, 3 dc in next ch-3 space, 2 dc in last ch-3 space, turn—20 dc.
Rows 2–6 Repeat Rows 2–6 of left neck shaping. Fasten off.

FINISHING

With right sides of front/back panels held together, whipstitch sleeve seams from last row of neckline to marked row. Determine which panel will be front of piece.

Lower Edging

Row 1 (Right Side) With right side of front panel Foundation Row facing, working in opposite side of foundation ch, join with slip st in first ch, ch 1, edging shell in next ch, [skip next 4 ch, edging shell in next ch] across, slip st in last dc, turn—21 (25, 29) edging shells.
Rows 2 and 3 (Slip st in first sc, ch 1-space, and first 2 dc) of first edging shell, ch 1, edging shell in center dc of each edging shell across, turn. Fasten off.
Repeat for Rows 1–3 for back panel.

Sleeve Edging (Work Twice)

Row 1 (Right Side) With right side facing, join with slip st in lower edge of sleeve, ch 1, work 17 edging shells evenly spaced across to seam, edging shell in seam, work 17 edging shells evenly spaced across remaining edge, turn—35 edging shells.
Rows 2 and 3 Repeat Rows 2 and 3 of Front Edging. Fasten off.

Neck Edging

Round 1 (Right Side) With right side facing, join with slip st in any seam, ch 1, work 14 (18, 22) edging shells evenly spaced around to next seam, work 14 (18, 22) edging shells evenly spaced around to first edging shell; join with slip st in first sc—28 (26, 44) edging shells.
Rounds 2 and 3 Repeat Rows 2 and 3 of Front Edging. Fasten off.

Weave in ends. Block to finished measurements, if desired. •

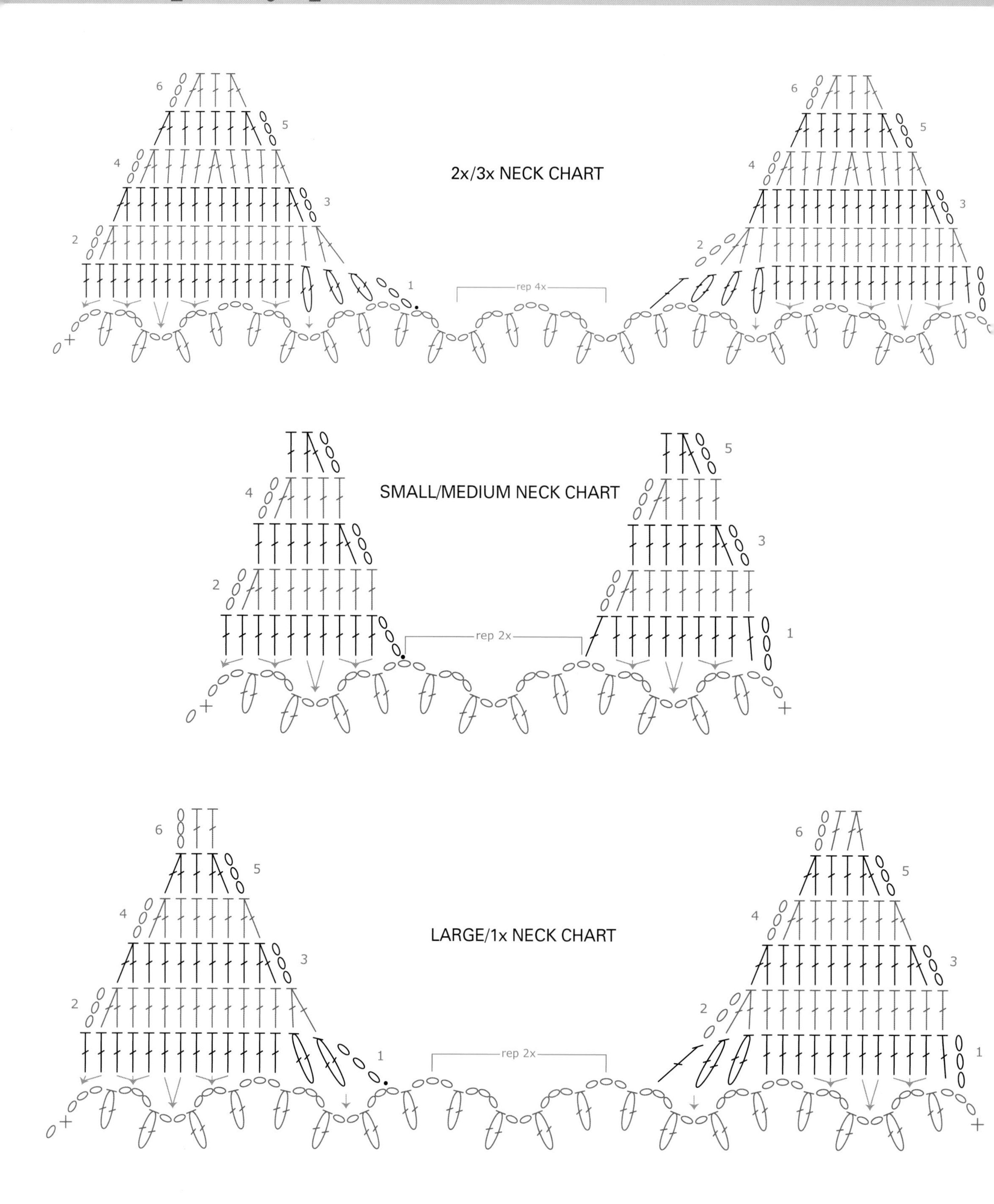
2x/3x NECK CHART
rep 4x
1
2
3
4
5
6
SMALL/MEDIUM NECK CHART
rep 2x
1
2
3
4
5
LARGE/1x NECK CHART
rep 2x
1
2
3
4
5
6

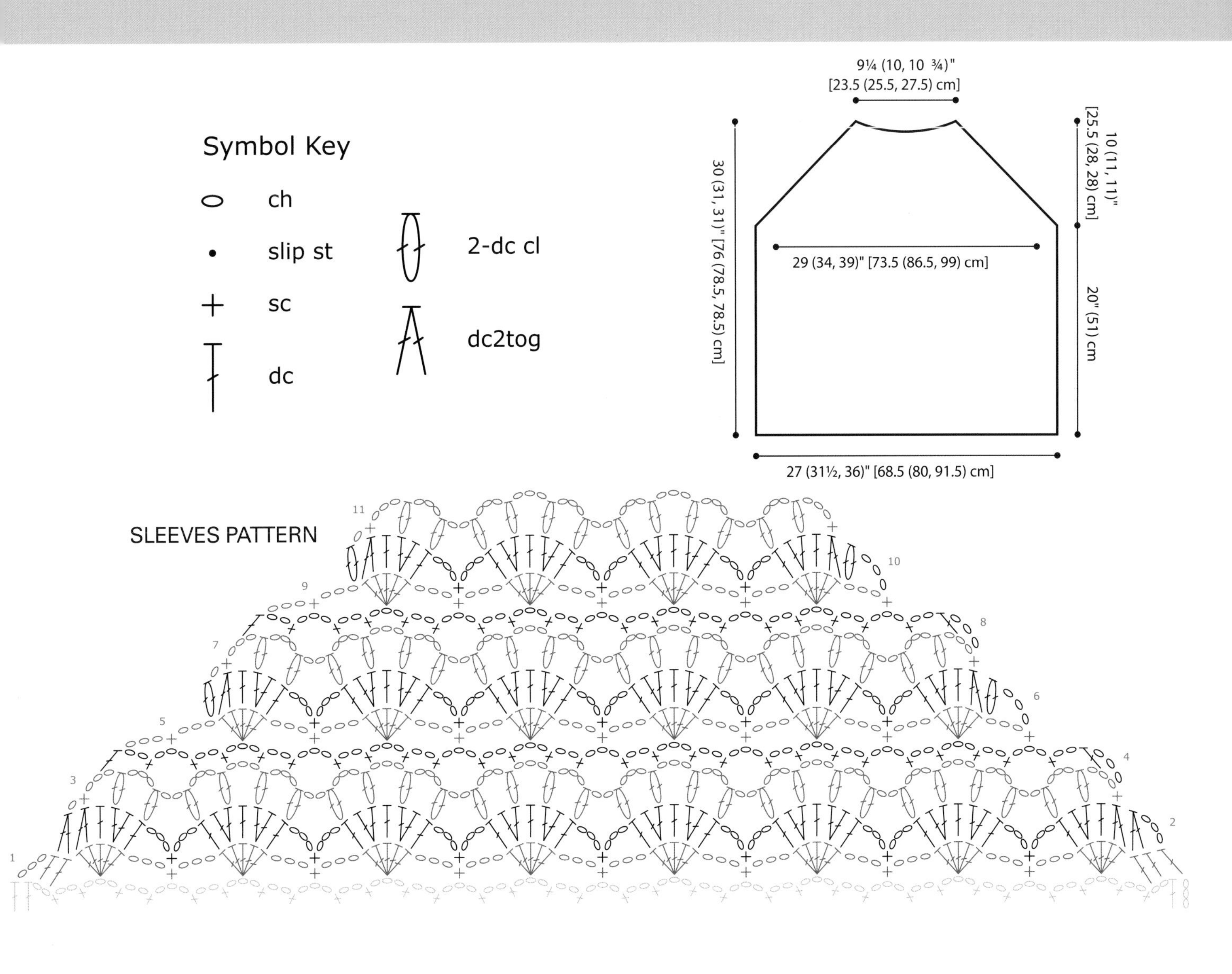
Symbol Key
ch
slip st
sc
dc
2-dc cl
dc2tog
9¼ (10, 10 ¾)"
[23.5 (25.5, 27.5) cm]
30 (31, 31)" [76 (78.5, 78.5) cm]
10 (11, 11)"
[25.5 (28, 28) cm]
29 (34, 39)" [73.5 (86.5, 99) cm]
20" (51) cm
27 (31½, 36)" [68.5 (80, 91.5) cm]
SLEEVES PATTERN

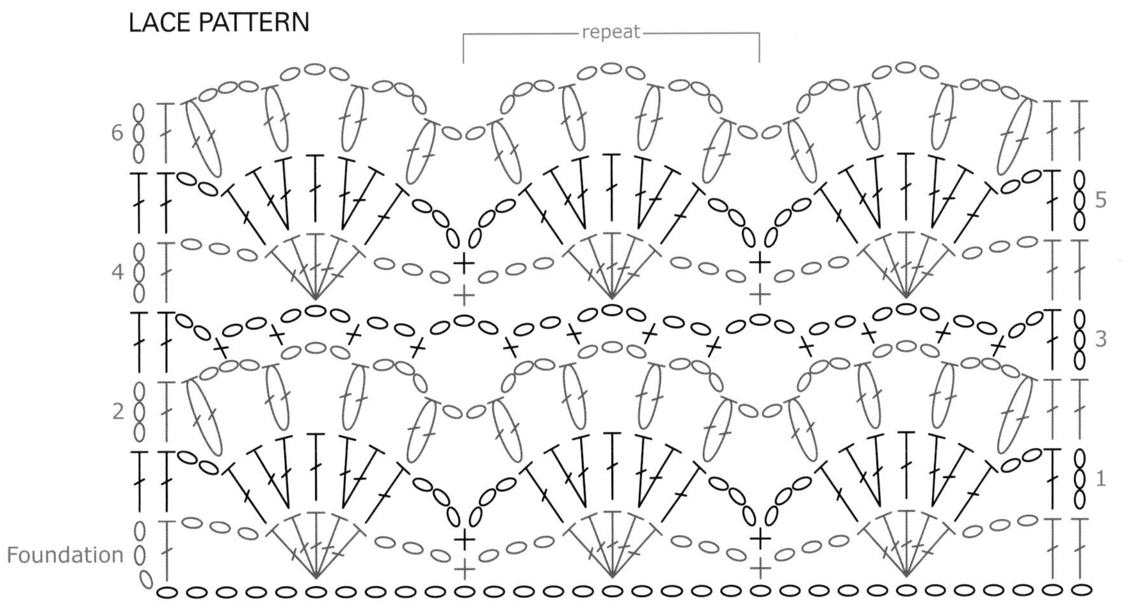
LACE PATTERN
repeat
Foundation

fringed poncho

Intermediate

MATERIALS

Yarn

RED HEART® Fashion Soft™, 5oz/141g balls, each approx 381yd/348m (acrylic) (3)

- 2 (2, 3) balls in 9440 Grey Heather (A)
- 2 (2, 2) balls in 4603 Grey Cream (B)
- 1 ball in 4614 Black (C)

Crochet Hook

- Size G-6 (4mm) crochet hook, *or size to obtain gauge*

Notions

- 2½"/6.5cm wide piece of cardboard
- Yarn needle

SIZES

Small/Medium (Large/Extra Large, 2X/3X).

FINISHED MEASUREMENTS

Body circumference 56 (64, 66½)"/142 (162.5, 169)cm

Length 20 (22, 23)"/51 (56, 58.5)cm

GAUGE

18 hdc = 4"/10cm; 13 rows = 4"/10cm using size G-6 (4mm) crochet hook.

CHECK YOUR GAUGE.

Use any size hook to obtain gauge.

NOTES

1) Poncho is worked from the top down in hdc.

2) On 2-color rows, carry the yarn that is not used along and crochet over it with the working yarn.

3) Do not turn work when working in the round. All rounds are worked with right side facing.

4) To change color, work last stitch of old color to last yarn over. Yarn over with new color and draw through all loops on hook to complete stitch. Proceed with new color.

PONCHO

With B, ch 81 (91, 91).

Row 1 (Wrong Side) Skip 2 ch (counts as 1 hdc), hdc in 3rd ch from hook and in each ch across, turn—80 (90, 90) hdc.

Row 2 Ch 2 (counts as 1 hdc here and throughout), hdc in each of next 3 (4, 4) sts, *2 hdc in next st, hdc in next 7 (8, 8) sts, repeat from * to last 4 sts, 2 hdc in next st, hdc in each st to end, turn—90 (100, 100) hdc.

Row 3 Ch 2, hdc in each st to end, turn.

Row 4 Ch 2, hdc in each of next 3 (4, 4) sts, *2 hdc in next st, hdc in next 8 (9, 9) sts, repeat from * to last 5 sts, 2 hdc in next st, hdc in each st to end, turn—100 (110, 110) hdc.

Row 5 Ch 2, hdc in each of next 4 (5, 5) sts, *2 hdc in next st, hdc in next 9 (10, 10) sts, repeat from * to last 5 sts, 2 hdc in next st, hdc in each st to end, turn—110 (120, 120) hdc.

Row 6 Ch 2, hdc in each of next 5 (6, 6) sts, *2 hdc in next st, hdc in next 10 (11, 11) sts, repeat from * to last 5 sts, 2 hdc in next st, hdc in each st to end, turn—120 (130, 130) hdc.

Row 7 Ch 2, hdc in each st to end, turn.

Row 8 Ch 2, hdc in each of 5 (6, 6) sts, *2 hdc in next st, hdc in next 11 (12, 12) sts, repeat from * to last 6 sts, 2 hdc in next st, hdc in each st to end, turn—130 (140, 140) hdc.

Row 9 Ch 2, hdc in each of next 6 (7, 7) sts, *2 hdc in next st, hdc in next 12 (13, 13) sts, repeat from * to last 6 sts, 2 hdc in next st, hdc in each st to end, turn—140 (150, 150) hdc.

Row 10 Ch 2, hdc in each of next 6 (2, 2) sts, *2 hdc in next st, hdc in next 6 (7, 7) sts, repeat from * to last 7 (3, 3) sts, 2 hdc in each of next 2 sts, hdc in each st to end, turn—160 (170, 170) hdc.

Row 11 Ch 2, hdc in each st to end, turn.

Row 12 Ch 2, hdc in each of next 7 (4, 4) sts, *2 hdc in next st, hdc in next 7 (8, 8) sts, repeat from * to last 8 (3, 3) sts, 2 hdc in each of next 2 sts, hdc in each st to end, turn—180 (190, 190) hdc.

Row 13 Ch 2, hdc in each st to end, turn.

Row 14 Ch 2, hdc in each of next 8 (4, 4) sts, *2 hdc in next st, hdc in next 8 (9, 9) sts, repeat from * to last 9 (5, 5) sts, 2 hdc in each of next 2 sts, hdc in each st to end, turn—200 (210, 210) hdc.

Row 15 Ch 2, hdc in each st to end, turn.

Row 16 Ch 2, hdc in each of next 9 (5, 5) sts, *2 hdc in next st, hdc in next 9 (10, 10) sts, repeat from * to last 10 (6, 6) sts, 2 hdc in each of next 2 sts,

fringed poncho

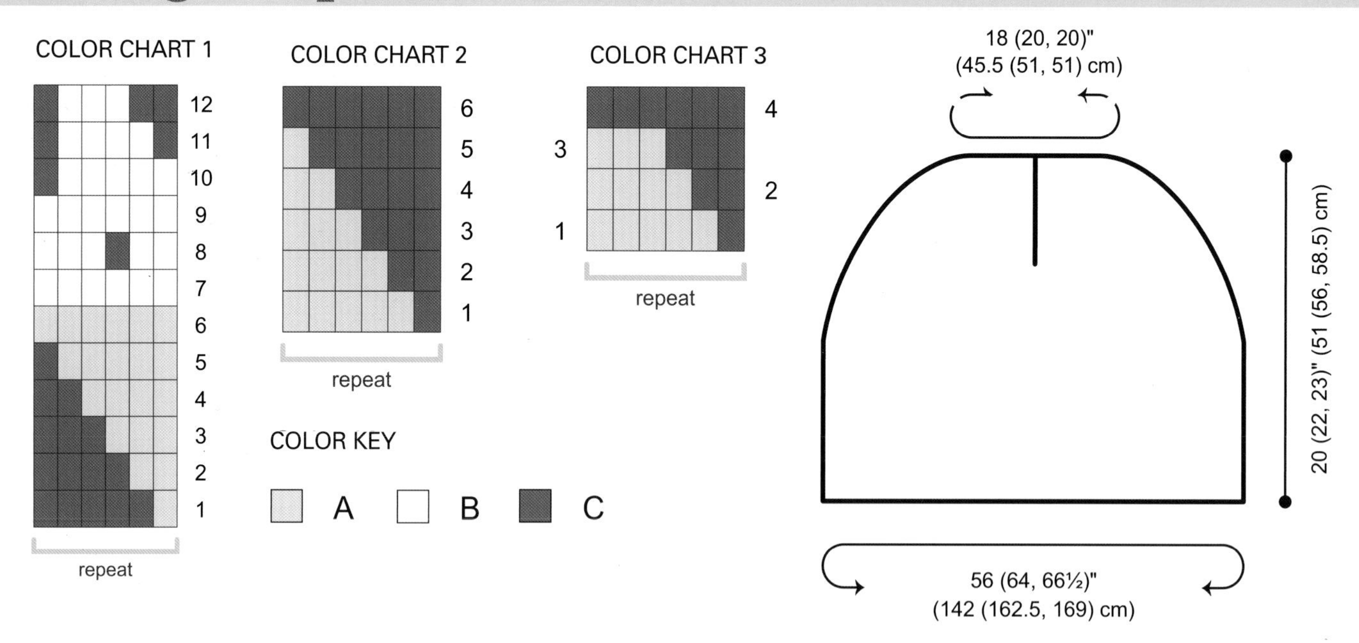

hdc in each st to end, turn—220 (230, 230) hdc.

Row 17 Ch 2, hdc in each st to end, turn.

Row 18 Ch 2, hdc in each of next 10 (6, 6) sts, *2 hdc in next st, hdc in next 10 (11, 11) sts, repeat from * to last 11 (7, 7) sts, 2 hdc in each of next 2 sts, hdc in each st to end, turn—240 (250, 250) hdc.

Row 19 Ch 2, hdc in each st to end, turn.

Row 20 Ch 2, hdc in each of next 19 (7, 7) sts, *2 hdc in next st, hdc in next 19 (12, 12) sts, repeat from * to last 20 (8, 8) sts, 2 hdc in each of next 2 sts, hdc in each st to end, turn—252 (270, 270) hdc.

For Sizes L/XL And 2X/3X

Row 21 Ch 2, hdc in each st to end, turn.

Row 22 Ch 2, hdc in each of next 7 (8) sts, *2 hdc in next st, hdc in next 14 (13) sts, repeat from * to last 7 (9) sts, 2 hdc in next 1 (2) sts, hdc in each st to end, turn—288 (290) hdc.

For Size 2X/3X Only

Row 23 Ch 2, hdc in each st across, turn.

Row 24 Ch 2, hdc in each of next 14 sts, *2 hdc in next st, hdc in next 28 sts, repeat from * to last 14 sts, 2 hdc in next st, hdc in each st to end, turn—300 hdc.

For All Sizes

Fasten off.

With right facing, count 126 (144, 150) sts over and join C with slip st next st.

Begin working in the round as follows:

Round 1 Ch 2, hdc in next st and in each st around, join with slip st in top of beginning ch-2.

Work 12 rounds evenly in hdc following color chart 1.

Change to A and work evenly in hdc until piece measures 18 (20, 21)"/45.5 (51, 53.5)cm from beginning.

Work 6 rounds evenly in hdc following color chart 2. Fasten off.

FINISHING

Collar

With wrong side facing, join B with a slip st at first st of top edge.

Row 1 (Wrong Side) Ch 2, hdc in each st across, turn—80 (90, 90) hdc.

Row 2 Ch 2, hdc in first st, *hdc in next st, 2 hdc in next st, repeat from * to last st, 1 (2, 2) hdc in last st, turn—120 (136, 136) hdc.

Rows 3 and 4 Ch 2, hdc in each st to end, turn.

Work 4 rows evenly in hdc following color chart 3.

Fasten off.

Tassels (Make 2)

Wrap B around cardboard piece 80 times.

Cut a 6"/15cm length of B, slip it between the cardboard and wrapped yarn, and tie it around the wrapped yarn at one edge of the cardboard.

Remove cardboard piece.

Cut another 6"/15cm length of B, and tie it around entire tassel ¾"/2cm below first tied piece.

Cut loops open at other end of tassel, and trim ends evenly.

With B, make a chain 30"/72cm long. Fasten off. Lace chain through edge sts at neck opening, then attach tassels to ends of chain.

Fringe

Cut 4 lengths of B, 10"/25.5cm each, and fold in half.

Using crochet hook, pull folded edge up through a bottom edge st just below a color A st (at the "point" of a color A wedge).

Pull ends through folded loop and pull to secure.

Attach a tassel in the same manner to every 3rd st along bottom edge.

Weave in ends. •